MAN
GROWN-UP®

Copyright © All rights reserved. ISBN 979-8-9944560-3-3

Man Grown-Up®

1. A man who practices living an authentic and joyful life.
2. Takes pride in progress.

www.ingramcontent.com/pod-product-compliance
Lightning Source LLC
LaVergne TN
LVHW070539070526
838199LV00076B/6808